TODAY'S 12 HOTTEST MOVIE SUPERSTARS

by Nancy Furstinger

12 STORY LIBRARY

www.12StoryLibrary.com

12-Story Library is an imprint of Peterson Publishing Company and Press Room Editions.

Produced for 12-Story Library by Red Line Editorial

Photographs ©: Rex Features/AP Images, cover, 1, 7, 16, 21, 25; Jaguar PS/Shutterstock Images, 4; Warner Bros. Pictures/AP Images, 5; Simon Burchell/Shutterstock Images, 6, 28; Disney Channel/Photofest, 8; Helga Esteb/Shutterstock Images, 9, 14, 17, 19, 26, 29; Paul Smith/Shutterstock Images, 10–11, 22, 24; AP Images, 12; Shutterstock Images, 13; Francois Duhamel/AP Images, 18; Featureflash/Shutterstock Images, 20; Columbia Pictures/Sony Pictures/AP Images, 23; James Bridges/AP Images, 27

ISBN
978-1-63235-019-0 (hardcover)
978-1-63235-079-4 (paperback)
978-1-62143-060-5 (hosted ebook)

Library of Congress Control Number: 2014946800

Printed in the United States of America
Mankato, MN
October, 2014

STORY
LIBRARY

Go beyond the book. Get free, up-to-date content on this topic at 12StoryLibrary.com.

TABLE OF CONTENTS

SANDRA BULLOCK: AMERICA'S SWEETHEART

Sandra Bullock's charm has earned her the nickname "America's sweetheart." Fans treasure her movie performances. Bullock started singing on stage at age five. After college, she moved to New York for acting lessons. She landed roles in TV movies, sitcoms, and B movies. Then she costarred in the movie *Demolition Man* in 1993. She did not earn praise for any of these roles.

Bullock's career took off in 1994 when she costarred in *Speed.* The movie zoomed to the top of the box office. It was a huge hit. Suddenly, Bullock topped Hollywood's A list. She starred in

Bullock stands with the Oscar she earned in 2010 for her role in *The Blind Side.*

In *Gravity*, Bullock plays a character who must survive the destruction of her space shuttle.

comedies such as *Miss Congeniality* in 2000. Then she starred in dramas such as *Infamous* in 2006. Next, Bullock tackled *The Blind Side* in 2009. This movie tells the true story of a homeless teenager who beat the odds to become a pro football player. Bullock gave one of the best performances of her career. She was rewarded with an Oscar. She was also nominated as best actress for the 2013 blockbuster *Gravity*.

CHARITABLE CELEBRITY

Bullock opens her wallet wide to help people. In 2010 she donated $1 million to Doctors Without Borders. This aided Haitian earthquake victims. She matched that amount the following year. Bullock gave $1 million to the American Red Cross after an earthquake and tsunami hit Japan. The actress also helped rebuild a high school in New Orleans, Louisiana, after Hurricane Katrina destroyed it in 2005.

5
Age at which Bullock began performing.

Birth date: July 26, 1964
Birthplace: Arlington, Virginia
Breakthrough Role: Lead in *Speed* (1994)
Top Accomplishments and Awards: Best Actress Golden Globe and Academy Award for *The Blind Side* (2009), Highest Paid Actress ($56 million) in the *2012 Guinness Book of World Records*

ROBERT DOWNEY JR.'S LIFETIME OF ACTING

Robert Downey Jr. played a puppy in his father's film *Pound.* That role kicked off a long acting career. Downey gained fame as a member of Hollywood's Brat Pack in the 1980s. This group of young actors starred together in many movies. Downey acted in *Less Than Zero, The Pick-up Artist,* and *Tuff Turf* with other Brat Packers.

All of the Brat Packers made headlines on and off the screen. Downey earned awards for his 1992 role in *Chaplin.* He nearly lost his career due to a struggle with drugs in the late 1990s. But he was able to turn his life and career around.

Downey had a swift comeback. He starred in small roles that showed off his acting ability. He also showed directors that they could trust that his drug problems were over. He joined the casts of *The Singing Detective, Zodiac, Shaggy Dog,* and *Good Night, and Good Luck.*

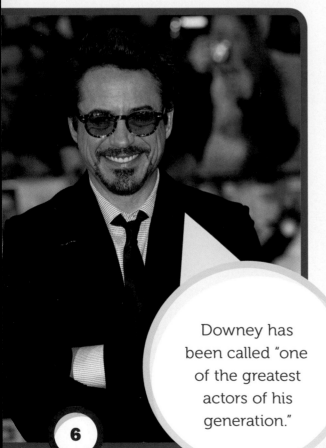

Downey has been called "one of the greatest actors of his generation."

1970

The year Downey acted in his first onscreen movie, at the age of five.

Birth date: April 4, 1965

Birthplace: Manhattan, New York

Breakthrough Role: Lead in *Chaplin* (1992)

Top Accomplishments and Awards: British Academy of Film and Television Arts (BAFTA) Award for Best Actor in *Chaplin* (1992), Golden Globe Award for Best Performance by an Actor in *Sherlock Holmes* (2009), People's Choice Awards for Favorite Movie Actor and Favorite Superhero in *The Avengers* (2012) and for Favorite Action Movie Actor in *Iron Man 3* (2013)

Next, the actor starred in blockbusters. In 2008, he played a comic book superhero in *Iron Man.* Downey continued the role in two sequels plus *Marvel's The Avengers.* The busy actor signed on to return as Iron Man in two *Avengers* sequels in 2013.

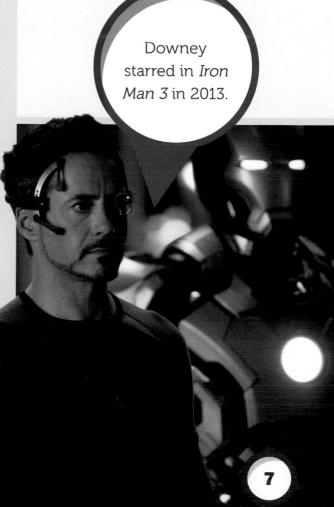

Downey starred in *Iron Man 3* in 2013.

ZAC EFRON HITS IT BIG WITH *HIGH SCHOOL MUSICAL*

Zac Efron starting acting at age 11. His singing voice helped him win a part in a school musical called *Gypsy*. Other stage roles followed. Then Efron guest starred in TV series. He landed a role in the TV movie *Miracle Run* in 2004. He played the character of a boy with autism.

In 2006, Efron starred in a TV movie that became a surprise hit. *High School Musical* broke records. It became

Efron jumped onto the scene with his role of Troy Bolton in *High School Musical*.

Disney Channel's highest-rated film. It also gave Efron a new role as tween star. Efron's singing voice was overdubbed in the show. But he did sing in the two *High School Musical* sequels.

In 2007, Efron sprang onto the big screen in *Hairspray*. Fans loved watching Efron act, sing, and dance. Efron soon signed up to star in the remake of the movie *Footloose*. But he dropped out of the musical. Efron did not want to be typecast. Instead, he starred in two romantic dramas, *Charlie St. Cloud* in 2010 and *The Lucky One* in 2012. Then he switched to comedy. In 2014, Efron starred as a college party boy in *Neighbors*.

In 2007, *Rolling Stone* magazine named Efron "the new American heartthrob."

11
The age at which Efron began acting.

Birth date: October 18, 1987

Birthplace: San Luis Obispo, California

Breakthrough Role: Troy Bolton in *High School Musical* (2006)

Top Accomplishments and Awards: Teen Choice Award for Breakout Star for *High School Musical* (2006), People's Choice Award for Favorite Dramatic Movie Actor (2013)

JAMIE FOXX: THE MULTITALENTED MAN

Jamie Foxx was born Eric Marlon Bishop. Eric showed many talents as a boy. He started playing the piano at age five. He later studied music in college. He also had a gift for comedy.

Bishop took his talent to the stage during open mic night at a comedy club in 1989. He found out that that female comedians performed before males at comedy clubs. So he changed his name to Jamie Foxx. Jamie could be used as a female or male name. Foxx enjoyed the applause he received as a comedian. He joined the comedy TV series *In Living Color* in 1991. Foxx quickly rose to the top as a comedian. Five years after his first role, he starred in *The Jamie Foxx Show*.

Next, Foxx launched his film career. He earned notice in the football drama *Any Given Sunday* in 1999. His background as a high school football player helped Foxx nail the role of quarterback.

In 2004, Foxx starred in two major films. He was nominated for Best Supporting Actor for *Collateral*. And he won the Oscar for Best Actor in the movie *Ray*. Foxx put to use his musical talent for his role as rhythm and blues legend Ray Charles.

Foxx proudly shows off his Oscar, which he earned in 2005 for his role in *Ray*.

FOXX'S MUSIC CAREER

In addition to his careers as a comedian and actor, Foxx also stars as a musician. He has released three albums. He also collaborated with Kanye West on two songs. One was "Slow Jamz'" in 2004. The other was "Gold Digger" in 2005, which won Foxx and West a Grammy Award in 2006.

2

Number of Grammy Awards Foxx has earned for his music career.

Birth date: December 13, 1967

Birthplace: Terrell, Texas

Breakthrough Role: Football player in *Any Given Sunday* (1999)

Top Accomplishments and Awards: Academy Award for Best Actor and the BAFTA Award for Best Actor in a Leading Role for *Ray* (2004)

DWAYNE JOHNSON: FROM THE RING TO THE BIG SCREEN

Dwayne Johnson starred in sports before he became a movie star. He played football, but wrestling was in his blood. In 1996, he joined World Wrestling Entertainment (WWE). Johnson made history as a WWE superstar. In the ring he was crowned "The Rock."

Johnson hosted *Saturday Night Live* in 2000. Afterward, Hollywood started calling. His first role was a bit part in *The Mummy Returns* in 2001. Then Johnson nabbed the

lead role in *The Scorpion King* in 2002. He earned $5.5 million for this role.

Johnson continued to attract attention in the ring and on the screen. He made audiences laugh in *Get Smart* in 2008 and *Tooth Fairy* in 2010. His role as an action star in 2011's *Fast Five* helped the film break box office records. He took up that role again in two more *Fast & Furious*

Johnson started his celebrity career as "The Rock," a WWE wrestler.

THE DWAYNE JOHNSON ROCK FOUNDATION

Johnson is on a mission to make kids around the world healthy. The foundation he started in 2006 aims to educate and help young hospital patients. With help from the foundation, these children take part in physical fitness programs. They also learn how to make healthy food choices.

movies in 2013 and 2014. Johnson showed off his strength in *Hercules* in 2014. He continues to star in movies.

$5.5 million

The amount of money Johnson earned for his lead role in *The Scorpion King*.

Birth date: May 2, 1972

Birthplace: Hayward, California

Breakthrough Role: Lead in *The Scorpion King* (2002)

Top Accomplishments and Awards: Kids' Choice Awards for Favorite Male Butt Kicker for *Journey 2: The Mysterious Island* (2013)

Johnson was the highest paid actor in 2007 for his first starring role in *The Scorpion King*.

6

MILA KUNIS TRANSITIONS FROM TV TO MOVIE

Kunis at the world premiere of *Oz the Great and Powerful* in Los Angeles, California, in 2013

Mila Kunis and her family moved from Ukraine to California when she was seven years old. She didn't speak a word of English. Mila learned quickly. She started acting at age nine. She soon landed small roles in TV shows.

Kunis lied about her age when she auditioned for *That '70s Show* in 1998. Actors had to be 18 years or older to be cast in the TV comedy. But Kunis was the perfect fit for her role as Jackie.

14

Age at which Kunis landed the role of Jackie in *That '70s Show*.

Birth date: August 14, 1983

Birthplace: Chernivtsi, Ukraine

Breakthrough Role: Hotel concierge in *Forgetting Sarah Marshall* (2008)

Top Accomplishments and Awards: Venice Film Festival award for *Black Swan* (2010), MTV Movie Award for Best Villain for *Oz the Great and Powerful* (2013)

A BELIEVABLE BALLERINA

Kunis had never danced before her role in *Black Swan*. The actress needed to train hard. She took ballet lessons for five hours a day for four months. All of her training caused Kunis to lose 20 pounds (9 kg) off her already thin frame. She suffered several injuries while practicing and filming. Kunis claims that she will never dance again.

The directors let her stay even after they found out she was only 14.

Kunis then shifted to the silver screen. Her break came in the 2008 comedy *Forgetting Sarah Marshall*. Kunis then won the key female role in the action film *The Book of Eli* in 2010. Her role as a ballet dancer in *Black Swan* in 2010 earned Kunis praise. She starred with Justin Timberlake in *Friends with Benefits* in 2011. And in 2012, she shared the screen with Mark Wahlberg and a teddy bear in *Ted.*

JENNIFER LAWRENCE BECOMES AN A-LIST MOVIE STAR

Jennifer Lawrence never took acting classes. But her parents told her she could try acting as soon as she finished high school. Jennifer studied hard and graduated two years early. She concentrated on her career and started landing acting gigs. In 2007 she was cast in the sitcom *The Bill Engvall Show.* She was off to California.

Lawrence became an A-list star after her role in *The Hunger Games.* As the heroine, Lawrence disappeared into the role of Katniss. The first two films in the series became instant blockbusters in 2012 and 2013.

Lawrence continued to land roles. She wasn't sure she'd win the starring role

Lawrence's role as Katniss Everdeen in *The Hunger Games* made her a star.

2013

Year Lawrence won an Oscar for her role in *Silver Linings Playbook*.

Birth date: August 15, 1990

Birthplace: Louisville, Kentucky

Breakthrough Role: Ozark Mountain girl in *Winter's Bone* (2010)

Top Accomplishments and Awards: Academy Award and Golden Globe for Best Actress in *Silver Linings Playbook* (2012), Golden Globe and BAFTA Award for best supporting actress in *American Hustle* (2013)

DOING WHATEVER IT TAKES

Lawrence nearly lost out on a big movie role because of her good looks. Producers thought she was too pretty to play the lead in *Winter's Bone*. So she showed up at the casting looking unkempt. Lawrence won the role of the teen searching for her deadbeat dad. She earned rave reviews for this indie film, which was released in 2010.

of the young widow in the 2012 comedy *Silver Linings Playbook*. She auditioned over Skype, and the director cast her. She teamed up again with Bradley Cooper in *American Hustle* in 2013.

Lawrence at the 86th Academy Awards in 2014

LUPITA NYONG'O EARNS PRAISE FOR ROLE OF PATSEY

Lupita Nyong'o was born in Mexico. She was raised in Kenya. There, she made her acting debut at age 14. A theater company cast her as Juliet in the play *Romeo and Juliet*. After she graduated from school in 2001, Nyong'o moved to the United States. She wanted to study film and theater.

Nyong'o worked in front of and behind the camera. But she preferred working in front of the camera. So Nyong'o attended the Yale School of Drama. There, she appeared in stage productions.

Nyong'o tried out for *12 Years a Slave* in 2012. She had not

Nyong'o as Patsey in the 2013 film *12 Years a Slave*

graduated from Yale. At the time, she was an unknown actress. Yet the director knew he had discovered his Patsey the minute he saw Nyong'o. The actress earned an Oscar for her film debut. Then she switched gears. She starred in the 2014 action-thriller *Non-Stop*. Next, Nyong'o joined the cast of the 2015 film *Star Wars: Episode VII*. Nyong'o now graces magazine covers. *People* magazine named her the most beautiful woman of 2014.

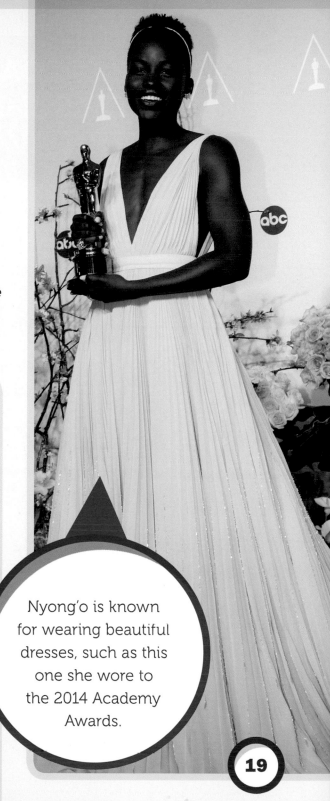

2014
Year Nyong'o was named *People* magazine's most beautiful woman.

Birth date: March 1, 1983
Birthplace: Mexico City, Mexico
Breakthrough Role: Slave Patsey in *12 Years a Slave* (2013)
Top Accomplishments and Awards: Academy Award for Best Actress in a Supporting Role for *12 Years a Slave* (2013), *People's* World's Most Beautiful (2014)

Nyong'o is known for wearing beautiful dresses, such as this one she wore to the 2014 Academy Awards.

19

ZOE SALDANA WINS FOR SCI-FI ROLE IN *AVATAR*

Zoe Saldana was born in New Jersey. Her father died when she was young. She spent much of her childhood living with her grandparents in the Dominican Republic. There, she sharpened her skills in ballet. Back in the United States, she joined a teen theater group.

Saldana at the 2011 Teen Choice Awards

Her first movie role copied her life. She played a ballet dancer in the 2000 film *Center Stage*. Next, Saldana showed off her range of acting skills. She acted in comedies, dramas, and thrillers. She attracted notice as a female pirate in *Pirates of the Caribbean: Black Pearl* in 2003.

Saldana played a series of strong females in blockbusters. She was the smart Uhura in the 2009 remake of *Star Trek*. That same year, she played Neytiri in *Avatar*. In 2014 Saldana starred in *Guardians of the Galaxy*. Saldana will return to play roles in planned sequels to these huge hits.

AN ANIMATED ACTRESS

Saldana played a 10-foot (3 m) tall blue alien warrior in the sci-fi film *Avatar*. This film was shot in 3-D, using a new technology called performance capture. It combines real actors with computer-generated animation. Saldana's ballet background helped her train for her demanding role. She also took up archery, horseback riding, and martial arts to help with her role.

2000

The year Saldana made her movie career debut as a ballet dancer in *Center Stage*.

Birth date: June 19, 1978
Birthplace: Passaic, New Jersey
Breakthrough Role: Ballet dancer in *Center Stage* (2000)
Top Accomplishments and Awards: ALMA Award for Favorite Movie Actress in a Drama/Adventure for *Colombiana* (2011), Academy of Science Fiction, Fantasy & Horror Films Best Actress for *Avatar* (2009)

Saldana scored an Academy Award for her role as Neytiri in *Avatar*.

EMMA STONE PLAYS STRONG FEMALE CHARACTERS

Emma Stone's real first name is Emily, but she prefers to be called Emma. Emma started acting in youth theater at age 11. When she was 15, she wanted to become a movie actor. Emma prepared a PowerPoint presentation. She called it "Project Hollywood." Emma's pitch convinced her parents she was ready for Hollywood. Emma and her mother moved to California. She was homeschooled while she auditioned for acting roles.

Stone got her first movie role in the 2007 comedy *Superbad.* She played the

Stone at the 17th Annual Screen Actors Guild Awards in Los Angeles in 2012

goofy sidekick in *The House Bunny* in 2008 and *Zombieland* in 2009. Then in 2010, she won the lead in

Stone played Spiderman's girlfriend Gwen Stacy in *The Amazing Spiderman 2* in 2014.

15

Age at which Stone convinced her parents she was ready for Hollywood.

Birth date: November 6, 1988

Birthplace: Scottsdale, Arizona

Breakthrough Role: High school student Olive in *Easy A* (2010)

Top Accomplishments and Awards: Teen Choice Awards for Movie Actress: Drama for *The Help* (2011) and Movie Actress: Comedy for *Crazy, Stupid Love* (2011)

the comedy *Easy A*. She then costarred in the 2011 films *Friends with Benefits* and *Crazy, Stupid, Love*. She became known for her strong female characters.

Stone's career quickly took off in new directions. She played a superhero's girlfriend in *The Amazing Spider Man* series (2012 and 2014). She took on the lead role of a writer in the 2011 civil rights drama *The Help*. And in 2013, she played a 1940s star in *Gangster Squad*. Her husky voice can be heard in the 2010 live-action *Marmaduke* and 2013 3-D cartoon *The Croods*.

CHANNING TATUM TAKES ON NEW ROLES

Channing Tatum had dreams of stardom as a boy. But he wanted to star in sports—not on the silver screen. He got a scholarship to play college football. But he dropped out.

Next, he worked odd jobs. He finally found success as a dancer and a model.

Tatum starred in a music video in 2000. In it, he danced to Ricky Martin's "She Bangs." This led to his first major film in 2006. He played a dancer in *Step Up*. He later repeated the role in *Step Up 2: The Streets* in 2008.

Tatum quickly proved he had movie-star charm. He played an action hero

2006

Year Tatum debuted on the big screen as a dancer in *Step Up*.

Birth date: April 26, 1980

Birthplace: Cullman, Alabama

Breakthrough Role: Troubled youth in *Step Up* (2006)

Top Accomplishments and Awards: Teen Choice Awards for Choice Summer Movie Star: Male for *White House Down* (2013) and Choice Movie Actor: Comedy for *21 Jump Street* (2012)

Tatum at the 2012 MTV Movie Awards

in two *G.I. Joe* movies in 2009 and 2013. In the 2012 romance film *The Vow*, he played a loving husband. Tatum told his own story as a dancer in the 2012 surprise hit *Magic Mike*. He switched to comedy in the 2012 film *21 Jump Street* and its 2014 sequel, *22 Jump Street*.

The leading man continues to take on new roles. His voice can be heard in *The Lego Movie* (2014) as the voice of Superman. He costarred in the 2014 wrestling movie *Foxcatcher*, as well as the 2015 sci-fi film *Jupiter Ascending*.

Tatum (right) starred with Jonah Hill in *22 Jump Street* in 2014.

SHAILENE WOODLEY BEGINS ACTING AT A YOUNG AGE

A talent agent spotted Shailene Woodley at a drama class when she was only five years old. Since then, Woodley has spent most of her life in the spotlight. She appeared in bit parts on TV shows. Then she landed the lead role in *The Secret Life of the American Teenager.* She played the lead character in the show from 2008 through 2013.

Next, Woodley starred in movies. She made her film debut in 2011 as a teen in *The Descendants*. Her acting attracted praise. Woodley then nabbed her first big screen role. She played Tris in *Divergent* in 2014. The actress will repeat her role in three sequels.

Woodley starred in another 2014 movie based on a young adult novel. The director of *The Fault in Our Stars* was not convinced Woodley should play the role of Hazel. However, two minutes into her audition, he was convinced she was perfect for it.

Woodley won the Independent Spirit Award for Best Supporting Female for her role in *The Descendants*.

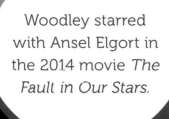

Woodley starred with Ansel Elgort in the 2014 movie *The Fault in Our Stars*.

5

Age at which Woodley was discovered as a star.

Birth date: November 15, 1991

Birthplace: Simi Valley, California

Breakthrough Role: George Clooney's teenage daughter in *The Descendants* (2011)

Top Accomplishments and Awards: Independent Spirit Award for Best Supporting Female for *The Descendants* (2011), crowned Female Star of Tomorrow at CinemaCon in 2014

BRACING AGAINST SCOLIOSIS

Doctors discovered Woodley had scoliosis when she was 15. Her spine curved from side to side. She wore a chest-to-hips plastic brace for two years. The brace worked and Woodley is now standing tall.

FACT SHEET

- Audiences watched thousands of silent films between 1890 and 1927. The first short films showed trains moving and animals playing. Later, films developed plots. They were shown in movie houses called nickelodeons. Tickets cost a nickel apiece. The films were accompanied by live music.

- New Jersey was the original movie capital of the world. Thomas Edison produced movies at his theater, the Black Maria, in West Orange. He shot more than 75 films there in 1894. These black and white films ran for roughly 20 seconds. Later, outdoor films were shot, including the popular *The Great Train Robbery.* The movie industry shifted to Hollywood, California, around World War I (1914–1918). Southern California has the perfect climate and landscape for shooting movies all year long.

- The first Academy Awards were handed out in Hollywood in 1929. The Academy of Motion Picture Arts and Sciences awarded 15 Oscars. That year, the first movie with sound—*The Jazz Singer*—was made. However, only silent films were allowed to compete for best picture.

- The Screen Actors Guild (SAG) was established in 1933. SAG was formed in Hollywood to give actors better working conditions. SAG stood up to the studio system. The major Hollywood studios in this system made many movies that netted big profits. Yet they offered actors unfair conditions, such as long-term contracts that they could not break. Today, SAG continues to fight for actors' rights.

GLOSSARY

A list
The most celebrated people, especially in show business.

audition
A short performance in which an actor tries out for a role.

bit part
A small role with few spoken lines.

blockbuster
A film that is very successful and earns a large amount of money.

B movie
A movie made with a low budget.

indie
An independent, low-budget film made by a small studio.

overdub
To add other recorded sound to a musical track.

sci-fi
Science fiction. A genre that often features space and technology.

sitcom
A situation comedy in which actors experience the same environment.

typecast
To repeatedly give an actor the same kind of role.

FOR MORE INFORMATION

Books

Albert, Lisa Rondinelli. *So You Want to Be a Film or TV Actor?* Berkeley Heights, NJ: Enslow, 2008.

Brooks, Riley. *All Access: Mega Movie Stars.* New York: Scholastic, 2010.

Foy, Debbie. *Teen Movie Stars.* London: Wayland, 2009.

Websites

The Actors Fund's Looking Ahead
www.lookingaheadprogram.org

AMC Filmsite
www.filmsite.org/oscars.html

SAG-AFTRA Young Performers
youngperformers.sagaftra.org

INDEX

About the Author

Nancy Furstinger is the author of almost 100 books. She has been a feature writer for a daily newspaper, a managing editor of trade and consumer magazines, and an editor for two children's book publishing houses. When Nancy is not writing, she enjoys watching movies with her pets.

READ MORE FROM 12-STORY LIBRARY

Every 12-Story Library book is available in many formats, including Amazon Kindle and Apple iBooks. For more information, visit your device's store or 12StoryLibrary.com.

32